WINE TYPES
Discover Your Inner Grape

Maureen Kelly

"As much about your inner self as about the world of wine, the enjoyable book 'Wine Types' gives a unique perspective on both."
- Michael Bishop
Senior Wine Buyer, Green's Beverages
Atlanta, Georgia

"Intelligent, fun and educational. Great for both the novice and the experienced wine drinker. A great addition for team building, social or wine education events."
- Jocelyn Whitton
Wine Consultant
E & J Gallo Winery Canada, Ltd.

"'Wine Types' is a small, simple book that is uniquely profound. It is another way of asking the question, "Who Am I?" While it entertains it asks you to look at yourself and how you interact with people and the world. I loved it and enjoyed reading it tremendously. I discovered I was a Merlot. What are you?"
- R. Nari Mayo
Author *Echoes of a Dream* and *True Heart*

"How entertaining...as a woman in the wine industry for many years this is a fresh perspective on not only wine and its history but your own personality."

- Diane Easterday Andrews
Samson Estates Winery, Everson, Washington

© 2009 Maureen Kelly

Third Edition

All rights reserved. No part of this book may be reproduced or transmitted in any form or by any means, electronic or mechanical, including photocopying, recording, or any information storage and retrieval system, without permission in writing from the Copyright owner. Address all inquiries to: sagebutterfly2@comcast.net (a division of sage butterfly design.)

ISBN: 1-4243-1814-9
ISBN-13: 978-1-4243-1814-8 **

This book is dedicated to all who seek
to learn more about themselves
and sip a little
(or a lot)
of wine along the way.

And to Genesis -
my sweet doggy.
You will always be by my side.

- Maureen

Genesis - Merlot

WINE TYPES
Discover Your Inner Grape

table of contents

Intro xi
Discovering Your Inner Grape................ 1
Wine Types Assessment 4
Assessment Results 8
Cabernet 9
Champagne 11
Pinot Noir 13
Merlot 15
Advantages & Stumbling Blocks 18
Pairings 28
Wine Type Under Stress 38
Wine Type Quests 40
Digging Deeper 42
Your Life Source 43
Choice 46
Basic Habits 49
Seasons Of Your Wine Type 53
In Conclusion... 54
Wine Type Seminars............................... 57
About Maureen 59
Recommended Reading 61
Additional Assessments......................... 63

"Limitless undying love which
shines around me like a million suns,
It calls me on and on across the universe."
- *John Lennon "Across the Universe"*

Thank you, John, for shedding your light.

"Across the Universe" was included on *No One's Gonna Change Our World*, a charity album released in the UK in December 1969 for the benefit of the World Wildlife Fund.

INTRODUCTION - *Close To My Heart*

"As far as we can discern, the sole purpose of human existence is to kindle a light in the darkness of mere being."
Carl Jung, *"Memories, Dreams, Reflections"*, 1962

My goal in writing this book was a lighthearted approach to a serious subject: *communication*. Increased self-knowledge can have a pronounced ripple effect between partners, among families, co-workers and even communities. If we nurture our growth as the winemaker his vines, with patience and caring, the results can only be positive.

My years working with both groups and individuals seeking to better know themselves as well as understanding the behavior of others 'in their bunch' has brought me much joy.

Another area of my life that inspires me on a daily basis is my interaction with my "4-legged kids". The unconditional love they share, their ability to live for the moment, and the enjoyment they find in simplicity are all wonderful reminders for us "2-leggeds" as well.

In an effort to celebrate these critters, a percentage of all Wine Types proceeds will be donated to two organizations that I hold in highest esteem for their contributions to our animal companions: The Whatcom Humane Society and Old Dog Haven.

The Whatcom Humane Society (WHS) has been caring for animals throughout Whatcom County since 1902. As the oldest non-profit animal welfare organization in Whatcom County, WHS is committed to caring for any animal in need.

Penny Cistaro, Executive Director
Whatcom Humane Society,
Bellingham, WA
www.whatcomhumane.org

Maya - Pinot Noir

OldDog Haven is a very small group of people with a network of foster homes and supporters. We aspire to provide a loving, safe home for senior dogs abandoned at this stage of their lives. Our goal is that their last years are happy and peaceful, knowing they are loved. Wouldn't we all wish this for our own pets, and for ourselves?

Judith Piper, Executive Director
OldDog Haven, Arlington, WA
www.olddoghaven.org

"Until he extends his circle of compassion
to include all living things,
man will not himself find peace."
-Albert Schweitzer

Lord, make me an instrument of Your peace.
Where there is hatred, let me sow love;
where there is injury, pardon;
where there is doubt, faith;
where there is despair, hope;
where there is darkness, light;
and where there is sadness, joy.
- *Prayer of St. Francis of Assisi*

Wine Types
Discover Your Inner Grape

It all starts with the vine. Combine the vine with the life force of the sunlight it receives, the quality of the soil where it is planted and new buds form. Wine is in the making.

Where do *you* grow best? What is your lifesource? What makes you who you are?

Nature vs Nurture... Terroir vs Winemaker

(In French, 'terroir' refers to "soil" and the inherent character of the earth that influences the taste of the wine.)

We are all born with certain innate characteristics that are then shaped to some extent by our environment. Just as a winemaker can alter the viticultural process by using different kinds of containers and temps during fermentation, adjusting how long a wine is allowed to mature and so on, the success of the wine itself will be dependent on whether that particular varietal is suited to the environment in which it is grown.

You would not, for instance, grow Chardonnay grapes, though immensely popular, in a land and climate inconducive to that particular grape.

You have probably noted times when you are involved in an activity compatible to your nature and time seems to fly, energy seems endless. There is just a unique fit.

But for those of us in a job, for example, that is requiring us to be someone we are not, the day will drag. A nap seems possibly the best solution. A realllllyyyy longgg napppp...

Many times we may actually be aware of what DOESN'T appeal to us, but we aren't quite sure how to replace it.

So the lesser of the two evils becomes stagnation, staying with what you already know. Ho Hum.

Here is where learning about your niche - your "Wine Type"- can be of assistance. As certain types find satisfaction in certain areas, this can at least put you on the right road.

As an example, if you become a doctor because that is the profession of your father and your father's mother and you are just expected to follow in this mold when you would much prefer being a concert pianist, the seeds are, needless to say, being planted in the wrong terrain.

This is one of the reasons learning about ourselves and the importance of our inherent nature can make the path of life a bit less rocky. (And hopefully a heck of a lot more fun.)

So, discovering your **'inner grape'** is a way of looking at who we are and which varietal we most resemble.

First let me give you a brief overview of how we will determine your Wine Type. We tend to possess certain attributes basic to all varietals, but you will probably find a 'comfort zone' - a more fitting fit - in one of the areas we will be covering.

Later, we will dig deeper to learn more about other aspects that will influence your Wine Type i.e. what energizes you, whether you are influenced more by your heart or your head and a look at your basic habits.

But for now, let's get back to the roots: Your Wine Type.

> Excellent wine generates enthusiasm. And whatever you do with enthusiasm is generally successful."
> - *Phillippe de Rothschild*

It is important to understand that when you fill out the assessment to identify your own particular Wine Type, your results will be determined based on the characteristics of a varietal and not necessarily the type of wine you prefer to drink.

Determining your Wine Type - the core of your personality. After checking off the characteristics in four separate categories that most apply to you, we will be looking at:

Cabernet, Champagne, Pinot Noir and Merlot.

After we determine your niche, we will then look at the **advantages and stumbling blocks** associated with your Wine Type as well as **pairings** with other types, your Wine Type under **stress** and your **quest** in life.

So kick back.. pour yourself a glass (or two)... and get ready to learn more about your "Inner Grape."

A simple choice.

Check the boxes on the following pages that most closely describe you.

CATEGORY 1 - ORDER

☐ Punctuality is very important to me.

☐ I tend to be very orderly.

☐ My friends know they can depend on me.

☐ I study the pros and cons before decision-making.

☐ I love to make lists and cross things off.

☐ I take commitments seriously.

☐ I enjoy detail work.

☐ I like to belong to clubs & organizations.

☐ I appreciate a structured environment.

☐ My motto could be "If it ain't broke, don't fix it."

☐ I follow Murphy's Law... if it can go wrong, it probably will.

☐ I am not crazy about change.

Total boxes checked: _____

CATEGORY 2 - RISK

- [ ] I adapt easily to new situations.
- [ ] I tend to live in the "now" and don't much like plans.
- [ ] I am a negotiator by nature.
- [ ] I get bored easily.
- [ ] I enjoy a fast pace.
- [ ] I'm not crazy about commitment.
- [ ] I like to take risks.
- [ ] I am good at putting out fires and enjoy the challenge.
- [ ] I sometimes appear unpredictable.
- [ ] I handle emergency situations well.
- [ ] I tend to be impulsive.
- [ ] I may have 10 things going at once, but am not always great with completion of task.
- [ ] I am a "free spirit".

Total boxes checked: _____

CATEGORY 3 - INDEPENDENCE

- [ ] I value independence.
- [ ] I am a skeptic by nature.
- [ ] I can appear cool or arrogant.
- [ ] No matter how good something is, I can improve on it.
- [ ] The conception of an idea is more fun than the follow through.
- [ ] I seek competence in myself and others.
- [ ] I have an unquenchable thirst for knowledge.
- [ ] I say "change for the sake of change!"
- [ ] If I see a button, I'll probably push it. ("Wonder what THIS does?")
- [ ] I'm always asking why...
- [ ] I enjoy playing devil's advocate.
- [ ] I am intrigued by a good riddle.
- [ ] I work well with ideas and concepts.

Total boxes checked: _____

CATEGORY 4 - ALTRUISM

- ☐ I am normally a good listener.
- ☐ I am an idealist by nature.
- ☐ I would like to make a difference in the world.
- ☐ I am drawn to careers that help people.
- ☐ Conflict makes me very uneasy.
- ☐ I am sensitive to criticism.
- ☐ I want to please "all the people all the time."
- ☐ I say "yes" sometimes when I really feel like saying "no".
- ☐ I search for the meaning of life.
- ☐ I am good at generating alternatives.
- ☐ I enjoy artistic endeavors: acting, writing, etc.
- ☐ I am prone to daydreaming.
- ☐ I don't like dealing with detail.

Total boxes checked: _____

Now review how many boxes you checked in each category. The category with the highest number of checks will correlate to your Wine Type. (If you choose, you can either sing, hum or just imagine the "Jeopardy" tune as you calculate).

While we are all a combination of these types to some degree, we normally have a comfort zone - a type that just 'feels right.' So if you have a tie in the number of boxes you checked, ask yourself which type has the best fit.

When you are done counting, just turn the page and learn your results.

Good Wine...
Good Friend...

It doesn't get any better.

(Nick-Cabernet)

If you checked more boxes in Category 1 (Order) your wine type is:

CABERNET...

TRADITIONAL - yet dependable, as with the Cabernet grape which is considered to be the easiest to grow and harvest - and plays by the rules.

REALISTS... You tend to trust your past experience over your gut feelings.

PREFER a strong foundation... while you will accept change, you would rather be the one to initiate it. You know that things have a correct order for life to run smoothly.

LIKE TO BELONG...Marching to the beat of a different drummer is probably not your style. Career choices might include managers, doctors, lawyers...

MURPHY'S LAW could apply here.... you may have a tendency to exaggerate the probability of things going wrong.

> *God in His goodness sent the grapes, to cheer both great and small; little fools will drink too much, and great fools not at all.*
> *- Anonymous*

About the CABERNET Varietal:
The Ambassador of Bordeaux

Cabernet Sauvignon is the name of both the grape as well as the wine it produces. Known as one of the world's finest red wines, its depth of complexity and richness of flavor give this grape a **sturdy foundation**. Cabernet is grown all over the world - South America, Australia, Northern California, New York... and of course France. The grape is very durable and adapts to various climates well. (It takes commitment seriously.)

One reason Cabernet is such a success in Bordeaux is that it has always been prized for its resistance. "Cabernet Sauvignon is a wine for people who like to sleep on the ground, play rugby, climb mountains, and eat Brussels sprouts." (Pride of the Wineries, California guide book).

"If it ain't broke, don't fix it." Cab prefers the status quo to change if things seem "just fine."

Also for your enjoyment: Cabernet is a great match for brie, cheddar cheese and chocolate.

Francesca - Cabernet

If you checked more boxes in Category 2 (Risk) your wine type is:

CHAMPAGNE...

LIVE FOR NOW - just as Champagne is made to be drunk upon opening as opposed to being aged, you also make the most of the moment.

SHORT ATTENTION SPAN... Like the bubbles making their way skyward... Poof. Gone.

NOT CRAZY ABOUT COMMITMENT... you probably prefer to pencil things in on your calendar (if you even use a calendar) in case "something better comes up."

LIKE ACTION... in your life as well as in your career - an environment where change is the rule rather than the exception. (If you are currently in a position where your days are routine, you are most likely quite frustrated.)

HANDS ON.... you probably prefer a real experience over theory.

CHAMPAGNE OBSERVATIONS...

"I am drinking stars!"
- *Dom Pierre Perignon*

"It tastes as though my foot's asleep."
- *Cole Porter*

About CHAMPAGNE...

OK... you got me on this one. It's just that this particular personality type can best be represented by what comes to mind when we think of Champagne: the person you want at your next party, the spur-of-the-moment guy or gal who will take a risk, go with you to Europe on a whim, and basically enjoy life for what it is.

It has toasted millions of celebrations, christened maiden voyages of countless ships and been a special part of evenings shared between just two.

But let's get to some of facts surrounding the origin of Champagne. Because the label 'real' Champagne should actually be reserved for the sparkling wine made in the French region of Reims (not far from Paris) our referral of 'champagne' to all of our own sparkling wines is sometimes dubbed a misnomer.

But where did it all originate? Around 1700, a blind French monk named Dom Pierre Perignon first tasted Champagne when he came upon a cask in which an accidental fermentation had occurred, tasted the bubbly product and declared, "I am drinking stars!" Whether this story is indeed true, the original Dom Perignon did most likely play a huge role in the development of Champagne.

Champagne is the wine of joy and festivity. Bubbly, personable, and ready to live life 'un-corked.' But (yes there is a but) the longevity is very limited... Uncork it and drink it now... it won't wait.

Jack - Champagne

If you checked more boxes in Category 3 (Independence) your wine type is:

PINOT NOIR...

PERFECTIONIST...You may tend to be a tough judge when it comes to standards that are up to your approval - either for yourself or others.

IF IT CAN BE IMPROVED ON... you will improve on it (or let it be known there is room for betterment.)

WHY? WHY? WHY?... You probably prefer to have things proved to you rather than accepting them on blind faith.

MAY APPEAR COOL OR ALOOF... as this grape variety prefers cooler climates you may have an aura of coolness when your mind is just otherwise occupied.

VISIONARY... Like the Pinot Noir Grape making large strides in the world of wine, you, too, enjoy the cutting edge.

CONNOISSEUR, n. A specialist who knows everything about something and nothing about anything else.

* * * * * * * * *

An old wine-bibber having been smashed in a railway collision, some wine was poured on his lips to revive him. "Pauillac, 1873," he murmured and died.
--"The Devil's Dictionary," 1911."

About the PINOT NOIR Varietal

While grown in diverse locations around the world, this grape is normally most recognized in the Burgundy region of France. Oregon is also now noted for its awesome production of Pinot Noir.

Pinot Noir is one of the most difficult grapes to grow and make into fine wine. It is also one of the very best when it is done properly. It has very specific requirements for its growing conditions. It needs warm days and cool nights. If Pinot Noir receives too little heat in the growing season, its wines are thin and pale. If the growing season is too warm, the wines have an overripe, cooked flavor.

Like the Pinot Noir personality type, it seeks perfection...and will test and prod the ordinary in quest of making it superior.

With the huge range of bouquets, flavors, and textures that Pinot Noir offers, this sometimes confuses tasters. Typically the wine tends to be of light to medium body with an aroma reminiscent of black cherry, raspberry or currant.

Difficult yet admired by wine lovers everywhere...

Simba - Pinot Noir

If you checked more boxes in Category 4 (Altruism) your wine type is:

MERLOT...

PERSONABLE...You enjoy communicating with others and like giving and receiving attention.

VULNERABLE TO WANTING TO PLEASE all the people all the time. As with Merlot which can be drunk with virtually anything, you also have a tendency to bend to accommodate others (sometimes too far).

YOUR HEART probably rules your head in most situations.

IDEALIST... you probably would like to 'make a difference in the world' and tend towards careers that involve counseling, teaching or artistic endeavors.

CONFLICT... is a dirty word. You avoid it whenever possible.

CONSTRUCTIVE CRITICISM .... is an oxymoron. Criticize a Merlot Wine Type and they will probably be hurt.

MERLOT TYPES... saving the world one person at a time.

"I cook with wine; sometimes I even add it to the food." --- W. C. Fields

About the MERLOT Varietal

What is it about Merlot that makes it so popular? In just over ten years, Merlot has gone from being a relative unknown to becoming the world's most popular red wine.

While originally mostly used as a blender to take the tannic edge off some more aggressive Cabernet Sauvignons, wine consumers are finding it to be a much more 'friendly' wine than Cab in terms of tannins and enjoyed for its fruitiness and drinkability. Here was a wine the consumer could pick up at the supermarket and drink that same evening with dinner.

Produced primarily in France, Italy and California, Merlot continues to spread its influence. Back in 1985 there were fewer than 2,000 acres in California. By 2003, there were more than 50,000. The softness combined with early ripening makes it a favorite for wine drinkers as well as the wine makers.

So, whether it's because you can pick it up at your corner store and drink it as soon as you get home or due to white wine drinkers switching to red for health benefits, the mellow, smooth bodied Merlot is an easy transition for anyone looking to appreciate red wine.

Easy to drink... easy to blend... amicable.

Chica - Merlot

It is well to remember that there are five reasons for drinking:

... the arrival of a friend
... one's present or future thirst
... the excellence of the wine....

or any other reason.

- Latin Saying

Advantages
&
Stumbling Blocks
(Heart Blockages)

There are advantages and stumbling blocks to each of our Wine Types. The advantages are innate personality traits, that when embraced, allow us to become easily proficient in certain areas, allowing our talents to shine.

Acknowledgement of the advantages brings an awareness that enables us to use them with greater frequency. The benefit from realizing the strengths inherent within these characteristics can increase the success and satisfaction we each experience along our life path.

The 'stumbling blocks' are those areas that we avoid - either consciously or not - because they challenge us to behave or react in a manner that brings some level of discomfort. Dodging responsibility to avoid this discomfort can thwart our progress in life. Once again, awareness of *these* areas can help us to come face to face with them and turn those challenges into benefits leading to greater happiness.

From a very early age events transpire in each of our lives that challenge us. The pain they often cause can get tucked away in the recesses of our heart and be triggered, sometimes quite unexpectedly, by incidents much later in life. This may at times cause us to wonder why the strong reaction to something possibly so mundane? We may also then recognize an avoidance game we have been playing without even realizing it.

If our happiness is dependent on life unfolding according to our own personal screen play, we are setting ourselves up for disappointment. As change is the only thing we can ultimately depend on, control is an illusion at best. As soon as we become 'friends' with that concept, our load becomes lighter, the path clearer.

It is indeed our reaction to what happens that either closes or opens our heart creating a "heart blockage" (stumbling block) or allowing life energy to flow freely (advantage).

Let's look now at each of the individual Wine Types and see how the advantages can streamline our lives and how the heart blockages /stumbling blocks can derail our progress.

" I like how wine continues to evolve, like if I opened a bottle of wine today it would taste different than if I'd opened it on any other day, because a bottle of wine is actually alive. And it's constantly evolving and gaining complexity."

- *Maya as quoted from movie "Sideways"*

CHARACTER
Advantages & Stumbling Blocks of the CABERNET Wine Type

Advantages:

The structured part of the Cabernet personality instills feelings of confidence both in themselves and others.

Being able to come to closure, knowing how to 'wrap it up' can be a distinct advantage in keeping teams on track.

The Cabernet is a wonderful part of a group effort also because they can lay a foundation from which others can spring. Their dependability is solid. If they say they are going to be somewhere or do something you can pretty well count on it

Stumbling Blocks / Heart Blockage:

The need for order, closure, and stability can lead to expectations of how things 'should be', how people should act. Always coloring inside the lines and carrying these preconceptions can lead to inner turmoil and outer conflict.

Heart blockage: Growth stunt due to resistance of trying new things or approaching them from a fresh standpoint. Sometimes the hell we know seems safer than the fear of the unknown, so we stay in a painful situation to avoid change.

How to free up the blockage? Embrace newness with an open heart. Attempt to uncover the past occurrences that have lead to rigid parameters that currently exist in your life. Make greater use of the advantages mentioned above, dependability, coming to closure, etc but sprinkle the 'same old way' of doing things with fresh approaches - and don't let Murphy's Law haunt you (the belief that if it can go wrong, it will...)

A Cabernet Scenario

I recall a cartoon featuring the Lockhorn couple where he is sitting in his easy chair in the living room and she is standing in front of his chair saying, "We could settle this whole argument amicably if we'll both just admit that you are wrong."

CHARACTER
Advantages & Stumbling Blocks of the CHAMPAGNE Wine Type

Advantages:

Being highly flexible, the Champagne Type can adapt easily to new situations and unpredictable circumstances. They are also able negotiators when conflict arises between two opposing forces

Their quick-thinking, action-oriented nature makes them naturals for careers as emergency room doctors, fire-fighters or nascar drivers...Anything that engages their sense of living in the moment.

The Champagne is also the one to invite to your next party to insure a successful turnout. They have been known to turn a boring get-together into a rollicking good time.

Stumbling Blocks / Heart Blockages:

Living in the moment can be a joyful experience, but if the 'current moment' introduces something painful, it wont *be* fully experienced. It can get shoved down inside the heart to be instantaneously replaced by a NEW moment. (Poof - gone... but not really.)

Heart blockage: Chasing happiness... If it's not here, it could be there... or over there...

One emotion/experience needs to be completed or at least digested before another takes its place if a continuity or feeling of wholeness is to reside in our hearts. Refusing to acknowledge an occurrence because it's 'not fun' only allows it to fester at a deeper level.

So again, embrace your "advantages" - spontaneity, joie de vivre etc - but remember the sun also produces shadows and they need to be explored as well.

Two champagne wine types were on a bear hunting trip together. Heading down a bumpy country path, they came upon a fork in the road and a sign that read, "Bear left."
So they went home.

CHARACTER
Advantages & Stumbling Blocks of the PINOT NOIR Wine Type

Advantages:

The Pinot has the ability to weed out what is not 'necessary' and easily see the big picture. They can analyze a situation without getting bogged down in particulars which can streamline an undertaking.

The Pinot Noir can also challenge most anyone about anything on an intellectual level. Their constant quest for perfection in themselves and others will keep quality levels high and productivity fluid.

Stumbling Blocks / Heart Blockage:

The need for perfection can lead to incessant comparison of self to others. This desire to compete or prove one's self leads to doing things just for the sake of showing what one is capable of rather than for the joy of doing it.

If a Pinot's competence is questioned, everything else takes a back seat until that doubt is put to rest.

Heart blockage: Fear of ever being inferior leads to a life of constant competitiveness…where there are no equals only "greater" and "lesser" (when indeed we are all doing the best we can wherever and whatever that might be at the moment.)

Perceiving this otherwise becomes judgment. Doing our best, expecting successful outcomes and trying to improve ourselves are all worthwhile efforts until its taken to an extreme that leads to alienation or causes others to feel inferior.

A Pinot and a Merlot were on a camping trip. Upon arising the first morning they were under the distinct impression that a bear was visiting in the area. The Pinot grabbed his backpack and began putting on his running shoes. The Merlot looked at him and laughed. "You don't POSSIBLY think you can outrun that bear, do you?" To which the Pinot replied, "No, but I can outrun you and that may be all the situation demands."

CHARACTER
Advantages & Stumbling Blocks of the MERLOT Wine Type

Advantages:

The Merlot is the idealist of life, waiting to serve whatever cause is at hand.

They work extremely well with people and recognize talent, thereby bringing out the best in others. Empathy is a natural component of their life and this awareness of the feelings of others garners the respect that is the birthright of each human being.

Usually eloquent and warm-hearted, the Merlot is also very effective in getting others to cooperate in group efforts.

Stumbling Blocks / Heart Blockage:

The Merlot's need for everyone to be happy and "save the world" mentality can backfire when they don't feel that their efforts are being appreciated. This can eventually lead to anger as well as false assumptions regarding what other people are actually feeling.

Heart blockage: Need for approval that isn't always there can hinder accomplishing the good one sets out to do. If you act truly from the heart for the benefit of another, then the reaction (or lack of one) is unimportant, if the act is truly selfless. Merlot must also remind themselves that one can't always know the basis for another's behavior and should attempt to get over taking everything so personally.

In Conclusion...

To take true ADVANTAGE of our ADVANTAGES we must be willing to clear heart blockages. This is not always a simple task as they can be extremely deep-rooted, but the result is well worth the temporary discomfort.

It all boils down to living a life of freedom vs building constant barriers and bandaging old wounds to prevent pain. Freedom definitely merits this effort.

When thoughts ferment over time
they often mellow
like fine wine.
Preserving only memories
of glasses shared
'tween Thee and me.
  - Maureen

PAIRINGS

You say "Syrah" and I say "Shiraz"...

Learning about your Wine Type can lead to increased self-knowledge as well as a greater understanding of your personal motivations.

The other area where this knowledge can be of distinct benefit is in our communications with others.

We all share some characteristics with one another, but the extent of that common ground can vary considerably.

In this next section, we will be looking at each of the different varietals and how they 'blend' with one another.

There are advantages and disadvantages to being both like-minded as well as diverse. Seeing things from the same perspective can make for a smooth road, but if alternatives or "what if's" are never questioned, a road block could appear quite unexpectedly.

The opportunity to learn from others is one of the greatest gifts that can stem from diversity in personalities. But the key is understanding each other's motives and thought processes.

If we are to indeed educate one another, avoid what could become conflict situations and generally enjoy one another to the greatest extent, this knowledge is key.

So let's look at Cabernet, Champagne, Pinot Noir and Merlot and how they interact. (Think your glass of wine is empty.... maybe you should get a refill before we continue.)

CABERNET and....

Champagne: These two start with some basic similarities such as being in tune to detail and living in the moment but that is where the likeness usually ends. The Cab is typically PLANNING those moments while the Champagne will be reacting second to second. This could lead to frustration on both parts as the Cab could see the Champagne as flighty and irresponsible and the Champagne sees the Cab as uptight and boring. Champagne is also not too concerned with something of great importance to the Cab: closure. They are much more interested in action for its own sake. If that action happens to BRING something to closure, so be it.

What can they learn from one another? Cabs could maybe learn to lighten up a bit and leave some room for spontaneity and change. Champagnes could consider a list from time to time but need to actually follow it.

Pinot Noir: Oh-oh. Some very possible head-butting could result from this pairing. Cab is likely to stick with the status quo if it's working. Why stir the pot if it doesn't need stirring? At the same time, the Pinot LIVES to stir up the pot just to see what will happen. Just because. Cabs may see Pinots as arrogant and Pinots see Cabs as overly structured.

What can they learn from one another? Cabs: respect the analytical nature of the Pinot. You may become aware of a whole new perspective on things that could lead to some substantial "ah-HAs!" in life. And Pinots: Sometimes it's best not to mess with a good thing.

CABERNET and....

Merlot: These two may see eye-to-eye on many things as the Merlot seeks a peaceful even-keeled atmosphere and the Cab does their best to provide that. The conflict may arise, however, if the Cab holding fast to the status quo results in hurt feelings or lack of consideration for another's situation - a head vs. heart type of thing.

What can they learn from one another? Cabs: keep the 'human' aspect in mind. And Merlot: Sometimes sharing news that someone may not want to hear is still for the best. Try keeping the 'higher good' in mind, despite the discomfort of imparting disconcerting information.

Both my father and mother were Cabernets and keeping to a schedule was very important to them. They were visiting me in my Springfield, Virginia home one autumn and had planned a trip into D.C. It was pouring outside and they stood in my living room totally decked out in hats and coats, umbrellas in hand. I was on my way to work and announced that I would put our dog out back so that we could all leave. Dad looked at his watch and said, "Oh we'll take care of it. We're not leaving 'til 8:30." I looked at my watch and saw that it was 8:24. They would stand in full rain gear in my living room until the clock hit the half hour. (Gotta stick to the agenda.)

CHAMPAGNE and...

Cabernet: These two start with some basic similarities such as being in tune to detail and living in the moment but that is where the likeness usually ends. The Cab is typically PLANNING those moments while the Champagne will be reacting second to second. This could lead to frustration on both parts as the Cab could see the Champagne as flighty and irresponsible and the Champagne sees the Cab as uptight and boring. Champagne is also not too concerned with something of great importance to the Cab: closure. They are much more interested in action for its own sake. If that action happens to BRING something to closure, so be it.

What can they learn from one another? Cabs could maybe learn to lighten up a bit and leave some room for spontaneity and change. Champagnes could consider a list from time to time but need to actually follow it.

Pinot Noir: This pairing can in many instances get along quite well... though they come at similar ends through different means. Champagne's love of action can easily lead to competence in an area, though that is not the justification *for* that action. Pinot's thirst for competence will *lead* them to action in order to be the best they can be.

Pinot's need to dig deeper into the "whys?" of any- and everything could grate on Champagne's live and let live philosophy. ("Go ahead and ripple the waters but don't waste time figuring out WHY they are rippling...")

What can they learn from each other? Champagne: Working towards a goal with competence as the destination can be a satisfying as well as learning experience. And Pinot: Pushing yourself to ridiculous limits in your quest for perfection could possibly remove ever feeling the glow of accomplishment.

CHAMPAGNE and...

Merlot: To Champagne, Merlot's constant questioning of life and purpose can seem a bit nonsensical as they tend to see life as a moment-to-moment existence. Merlot may sometimes envy Champagne's ability to live for now and throw caution to the wind. Though if taken to an extreme, that envy may turn to disdain in the belief that the Champagne is living a "don't give a damn" lifestyle. With understanding, this pairing can lead to an event-filled, purposeful relationship: key word being 'understanding' and awareness of how each one goes about their daily existence. This is not a quest (as for all type pairings) to change the other into themselves. In this particular pairing, this would most likely stem from the Merlot thinking they were 'helping' the other fulfill their destiny.

What can they learn from each other? Champagne: Having a life purpose - or goals, for that matter - can greatly assist in channeling that energy you expend into tangible achievements. And Merlot: Understanding Champagne's need for freedom and action will keep you from constantly trying to 'reign them in.'

For Champagne, a long range plan is a contradiction in terms.

PINOT NOIR and...

Cabernet: Oh-oh. Some very possible head-butting could result from this pairing. Cab is likely to stick with the status quo if it's working. Why stir the pot if it doesn't need stirring? At the same time, the Pinot LIVES to stir up the pot just to see what will happen. Just because. Cabs may see Pinots as arrogant and Pinots see Cabs as overly structured.

What can they learn from one another? Cabs: respect the analytical nature of the Pinot. You may become aware of a whole new perspective on things that could lead to some substantial "ah-HAs!" in life. And Pinots: Sometimes it's best not to mess with a good thing.

Champagne: This pairing can in many instances get along quite well... though they come at similar ends through different means. Champagne's love of action can easily lead to competence in an area, though that is not the justification *for* that action. Pinot's thirst for competence will *lead* them to action in order to be the best they can be. Pinot's need to dig deeper into the "whys?" of any- and everything could grate on Champagne's live and let live philosophy. ("Go ahead and ripple the waters but don't waste time figuring out WHY they are rippling...")

What can they learn from each other? Champagne: Working towards a goal with competence as the destination can be a satisfying as well as learning experience. And Pinot: Pushing yourself to ridiculous limits in your quest for perfection could possibly remove ever feeling the glow of accomplishment.

PINOT NOIR and...

Merlot: These two have a basic foundation in that they see/relate to a bigger picture and a world of possibilities. Depending, however, on the nature of their dealings, they could hit a crossroads rather quickly. Merlot's quest for personal growth and desire to nurture could seem capricious and a waste of energy to the Pinot. "Yea, yea, that's very sweet but let's get back to reality." Merlot may see Pinot's equally determined quest for perfection as over the top. The idea that something can always be bettered can lead to feelings of inadequacy in relationships with others.

What can they learn? Pinot will be reminded of the human factor involved in their quest and respect for accomplishments of others and Merlot will see that some goals require that extra effort to realize their dreams.

A Pinot and a Merlot were sitting on their back deck reading the paper when the Merlot spotted an article about a man seeking 5 experienced people to sail his yacht from Europe back to the states. He ended up hiring the 5 without doing proper background checks. They were all fair sailors but not as knowledgable as needed be... A terrible storm came up, capsized the yacht and all 5 were killed.

The Merlot shook her head in dismay and said, "What a terrible waste of life! Had that man done proper research those lives need not have been lost!"

The Pinot said, "I sure hope he had insurance on the boat."

MERLOT and...

Cabernet: These two may see eye-to-eye on many things as the Merlot seeks a peaceful even-keeled atmosphere and the Cab does their best to provide that. The conflict may arise, however, if the Cab holding fast to the status quo results in hurt feelings or lack of consideration for another's situation - a head vs. heart type of thing.

What can they learn from one another? Cabs: keep the 'human' aspect in mind. And Merlot: Sometimes sharing news that someone may not want to hear is still for the best. Try keeping the 'higher good' in mind, despite the discomfort of imparting disconcerting information.

Champagne: To Champagne, Merlot's constant questioning of life and purpose can seem a bit nonsensical as they tend to see life as a moment-to-moment existence. Merlot may sometimes envy Champagne's ability to live for now and throw caution to the wind. Though if taken to an extreme, that envy may turn to disdain in the belief that the Champagne is living a "don't give a damn" lifestyle. With understanding, this pairing can lead to an event-filled, purposeful relationship: key word being 'understanding' and awareness of how each one goes about their daily existence. This is not a quest (as for all type pairings) to change the other into themselves. In this particular pairing, this would most likely stem from the Merlot thinking they were 'helping' the other fulfill their destiny.

What can they learn from each other? Champagne: Having a life purpose - or goals, for that matter - can greatly assist in channeling that energy you expend into tangible achievements. And Merlot: Understanding Champagne's need for freedom and action will keep you from constantly trying to 'reign them in.'

MERLOT and...

Pinot Noir: These two have a basic foundation in that they see/relate to a bigger picture and a world of possibilities. Depending, however, on the nature of their dealings, they could hit a crossroads rather quickly. Merlot's quest for personal growth and desire to nurture could seem capricious and a waste of energy to the Pinot. "Yea, yea, that's very sweet but let's get back to reality." Merlot may see Pinot's equally determined quest for perfection as over the top. The idea that something can always be bettered can lead to feelings of inadequacy in relationships with others.

What can they learn? Pinot will be reminded of the human factor involved in their quest and respect for accomplishments of others and Merlot will see that some goals require that extra effort to realize their dreams.

At a couple's workshop years ago, we were divided up into similar temperament groups and asked to "Define love." My group - the Merlot equivalent- came up with a list that included things like "The glue that holds everything together, caring, charity, sharing of ourselves, makes the world go round, etc." My ex-husband's group was made up of the Pinot Noir equivalent. When they revealed their definitions, at the top of the list was COLD FUSION. I IMMEDIATELY knew he was responsible for that addition... but then was actually quite speechless when he gave his explanation: "The more you put into it, the more you get out." Wow.
- *Maureen*

How Differently We Respond To Life Situations...

A Merlot, a Cabernet and a Pinot Noir were waiting one morning for a particularly slow group of golfers. The Cabernet fumed, "What's the matter with these guys? We have been waiting for over 15 minutes!"

The Pinot chimed in, "I don't know, but I've never seen such incompetence!"

The Merlot said, "Hey, here comes the greens keeper. Let's have a chat with him."

"Hi Sam. Say, what's with the group ahead of us? They're awfully slow!"

The greens keeper replied, "Oh yes, that's a group of blind firefighters. They lost their sight saving our clubhouse from a fire last year. We always let them play for free whenever they choose."

The group was silent for a moment.

The Merlot said, "That is really sad. I will say a special prayer for them tonight."

The Cabernet said, "Yes, I will as well. And I will also contact a good Opthamologist friend of mine. Maybe there is something he can do.

The Pinot said, "Why the heck can't these guys play at night?"

(Wondering where the Champagne is? He is already off partying in the clubhouse.)

Wine Types Under Stress

So how do YOU react under pressure? (Aside from pouring yourself a nice glass of vino if able...)

We typically become a pronounced version of our own individual Wine Type, that is, when stress levels are average.

But oh boy.... Should the levels of stress become extreme, that is a different story. You may start exhibiting characteristics of other Wine Types and not always in an attractive manner.

Let's take a gander.

CABERNET UNDER STRESS

Initially may become even more structured in an attempt to be/stay in control. As the level of stress increases, however, this Wine Type may throw caution to the wind and act uncharacterIstically "fly-by-the-seat-of-your-pants." This could be a shake up for all concerned, especially if taken to extremes.

CHAMPAGNE UNDER STRESS

Initially may become even more "Eat, Drink and be Merry." (You know the rest.) But as the level of stress increases, may search out structure and boundaries. For those of us accustomed to dealing with Champagne types, this is truly atypical and a warning sign of severe stress levels.

PINOT NOIR UNDER STRESS

Initially may become even more competitive, self-critical and terse in communication with others. As levels of stress continue to rise, however, you may witness a softening, almost "poor me" turn of behavior where the heart takes over the head. (Not always pretty.)

MERLOT UNDER STRESS

Initially may go into a mode of "Joan of Arc" and believe all will be well if they just try a little harder to fix what's broken. But then, if the levels of stress increase, they could turn cold and bitter, feeling as if the load of the world has been placed squarely upon their shoulders and no one is even attempting to help...

Recognizing these signs both in ourselves as well as friends and family can sometimes help to diffuse potential conflict, as the reasons for the seemingly "odd" behavior can be explained. This may not remove the CAUSE of the stress, but could make finding a solution more likely.

If each of the types had a motto, they might read something like this:

CABERNET: Support it.
CHAMPAGNE: Live it.
PINOT NOIR: Prove it (or *IMPROVE* it.)
MERLOT: Save it.

WINE TYPE QUESTS

In this adventure we call life, each of us has different callings and goals. Here is a brief recap of what each Wine Type might claim as their quest:

CABERNET: Tradition & Responsibility

CHAMPAGNE: Freedom & Action

PINOT NOIR: Independence & Competence

MERLOT: Self-actualization & Nurturing

"Writing in my sixty-fourth year, I can truthfully say that since I reached the age of discretion I have consistently drunk more than most people would say is good for me. Nor did I regret it. Wine has been for me a firm friend and a wise counsellor. Often...wine has shown me matters in their true perspective, and has, as though by the touch of a magic wand, reduced great disasters to small inconveniences. Wine has lit up for me the pages of literature, and revealed in life romance lurking in the commonplace. Wine has made me bold but not foolish; has induced me to say silly things but not to do them."
--*Cooper Duff - Old Men Forget*

"We hear of the conversion of water into wine at the marriage in Cana as of a miracle. But this conversion is, through the goodness of God, made every day before our eyes. Behold the rain which descends from heaven upon our vineyards, and which incorporates itself with the grapes, to be changed into wine; a constant proof that God loves us, and loves to see us happy."

-Benjamin Franklin

DIGGING DEEPER
Peeling the layers of your 'Inner Grape'...

As we have just taken a pretty comprehensive look at your Wine Type, we must also realize that other factors can influence our personalities and balance. We are going to explore the following three topics:

OUR LIFE SOURCE: What energizes you?
CHOICE: Do you go with your head or your heart?
BASIC HABITS: What is your framework for living?

By answering the questions on the following pages, you can come to even deeper understanding of your overall Wine Type.

When complete, you will have your core Wine Type with an influence from other varietals. For example, you could be a Pinot Noir with a Chianti, Sauvignon Blanc, Maderia influence. (Sound confusing? Keep reading... it will be clear soon!)

So get your pens ready (or pencils for those of you who change your mind a lot) and answer the questions on the next few pages. And let's learn even more about you.

"It's never too late to be who you might have been."
—George Eliot

YOUR LIFE SOURCE:
What energizes you?

What we could designate as our "Life Source" or where we get our energy greatly influences us.

For a vine, the amount of sunlight it receives as well as the quantity of rainfall will have a huge impact on its maturation process.

Just as some vines require more of each of these than others for optimal growth and vitality, some of us prefer *solitude* over *companionship* to be energized.

Answer the following questions to determine if you are a

CHIANTI or a RIESLING.

*"Always do sober what you said you'd do drunk.
This will teach you to keep your mouth shut."*
-Ernest Hemingway

1. When attending an event like a wine tasting, do you
   a) tend to meet a lot of new 'friends'
   b) stick more to yourself (yourselves)?

2. Which scene appeals to you more?
   a) a wine fest in a vineyard with lots of people
   b) a quiet evening in front of the fire with a good bottle of wine

3. Are you
   a) the first to know the latest, whether it be a new wine release or the talk of the town or
   b) is that kind of 'idle chatter' unimportant?

4. If you undertake a new venture, do you
   a) seek out the advice of others?
   b) just do it?

5. Do
   a) people generally know how you feel about things
   b) you tend to keep your opinions to yourself?

Total "a" answers: _____

Total "b" answers: _____

Turn to the next page to discover your *Life Source.*

If you had more "a" choices, you are **Chianti**.

Chianti doesn't show well by itself. But when paired with food, Chianti shines and is strong and bold tasting. With Sangiovese as its varietal base, these wines are constantly evolving, depending on where the grapes were grown and what, if any, additional grapes are blended with them.

This type gets its energy from being with others, likes to share their views and appreciates feedback. Sometimes plagued by engaging their mouths before their brains, they may also have a proclivity for speaking with their hands.

If you had more "b" choices, you are **Riesling.**

Rieslings are floral and fruity, and can be delicate, subtle, and low in alcohol, making for a very nice summer wine. But even sweet, low-alcohol wines from the Mosel in Germany balance the sugar with a steely, teeth-cleaning acidity. And though you might think of Rieslings as necessarily sweet, there are many dry Rieslings, the best being from Alsace. These show best with several years of bottle age--though they are certainly fun to drink young!

This type avoids the trendy and is energized by the conceptual, solitude and introspection. What you see is not always what you get as still waters run deep.

> *The meeting of two personalities is like the contact of two chemical substances: if there is any reaction, both are transformed.*
> *-Carl Jung*

CHOICE:
Do you go with your head or your heart?

As I mentioned earlier in the book, we all have our comfort zones.

There are those who are more inclined to empathize with others to the point of 'stepping inside their shoes' and therefore, being ruled by the heart.

And there are those who can indeed empathize, yet have the ability to disassociate themselves from the event, being more likely be ruled by their head.

(It's probably a wise move to attempt a combination of these two ways of behaving... and possibly pick up pointers from those who process things differently from ourselves.)

Answer the following questions to determine if you are a

SAUVIGNON BLANC or a SYRAH.

1. Do you consider wine to be a natural addition to a romantic evening?
   a) no
   b) yes

2. If you ordered wine in a restaurant that was unsatisfactory, would you
   a) return it
   b) just drink it and sulk a bit

3. Would you consider it an insult if someone corrected your pronunciation of a wine or a wine region?
   a) no
   b) yes

4. If a situation that is troubling you is out of your control, do you
   a) just move on and let it pan out
   b) worry about it anyway

5. If there was only enough wine left to fill one glass, would you
   a) drink it
   b) offer it to someone else

Total "a" answers: _____

Total "b" answers: _____

Turn to the next page to discover your method of *CHOICE*.

If you had more "a" choices, you are **Sauvignon Blanc.**

The **Sauvignon Blanc** grape produces wines of distinction in most of the areas where it is grown and can tolerate greater heat than many varieties. An assertive grape, most producers ferment and age their sauvignon blancs in stainless steel to accentuate the wine's crisp, zesty, bracing qualities.

This lifestyle tells it like it is and values objectivity and logic. They tend to have thicker skins and are more firm-minded than gentle-hearted. (Sharing much in common with the Pinot Noir Wine Type.)

If you had more "b" choices, you are **Syrah.**

Syrah is a rich, full-bodied, complex, spicy wine that thrives in the Rhone region of France. It is the most popular red wine in Australia (where it is called Shiraz and is often blended with Cabernet Sauvignon) and is becoming increasingly popular in California. Syrah can be successfully blended with many other wine grapes (often to give them more backbone and structure); it also can be made in a variety of styles ranging from soft and medium-bodied with some berrry characteristics to deeply colored and powerful, tasting of roasted peppers, black cherry and smoke.

This lifestyle values empathy, is service-oriented and shuns conflict. The Syrah lifestyle is vulnerable to wanting to please all the people all the time. (Sharing much in common with the Merlot Wine Type.)

BASIC HABITS:
What is your framework for living?

And for our last category, what about you and your basic habits? Do you appreciate having your life fairly well mapped out, always know where to find your keys, and get a little ticked if you are offered a red wine when you had your taste buds ready for white?

Or do you get up each morning allowing life to flow as it will, maybe starting three or four projects (possibly without finishing any of them) and think that being punctual means showing up at some point?

Well, answer the following questions to define whether you are a

MADEIRA or a CHARDONNAY.

Is it an enlightened state to know you are confused?

1. If you made a trip to a wine region, would you rather
    a) have a scheduled plan of activities?
    b) play it by ear?

2. If you were hosting a wine tasting, would you be concerned about matching glassware?
    a) yes
    b) no

3. If you are invited to an event, would you rather it
    a) be far enough in advance so that you have time to plan ?
    b) be spur of the moment?

4. If you had unexpected guests show up right before dinner, would you be very annoyed?
    a) yes
    b) no

5. Do you
    a) tend to buy the same wine all the time?
    b) like to experiment with new wines?

Total "a" answers: _____

Total "b" answers: _____

Turn to the next page to discover your *Framework For Living.*

If you had more "a" choices, you are **MADEIRA.**

MADEIRA is probably the most indestructible wine in the world. Historically, the wines were fortified with alcohol and then shipped by boat across the tropics in long sea journeys to the Americas. The wine became know as "vinho da roda" or "wine of the round voyage." The wine's name comes from the name of the island, a Portuguese possession in the Atlantic about 625 miles from Portugal. Used to toast the Declaration of Independence, this wine stands for stability.

This lifestyle thrives on order. Of importance in their lives are closure, lists and structure. (Having much in common with the Cabernet.)

If you had more "b" choices, you are a **CHARDONNAY.**

CHARDONNAY is America's number one selling white wine and continues to climb the production ladders as the most popular of dry white wines in the U.S. It is a relatively "low-maintenance" vine that adapts well to a variety of climates resulting in fairly high yields worldwide. Part of the attraction of Chardonnay, for wine makers and lovers alike, is its versatility.

This lifestyle values having a flexible schedule, living spontaneously and openness. One must also be aware of the "danger zone" with the Chardonnay lifestyle, as they can be quite easily distracted and tend toward procrastination. (Sharing much in common with the Champagne Wine Type.)

> A waltz and a glass of wine
> invite an encore.
> - *Johann Strauss*

While the following could be a "Champagne Observation" I think we can all learn something...

Life is not a journey to the grave with the intention of arriving safely in a pretty and well preserved body, but rather to skid in broadside, thoroughly used up, totally worn out, and loudly proclaiming "WOW - What a Ride!"
- *Unknown Source*

THE SEASONS OF YOUR WINE TYPE

PINOT NOIR:
Spring & What is new and different?

CHAMPAGNE:
Summer & Fun...

MERLOT:
Fall & Nostalgia - Time for Reflection...

CABERNET:
Winter & Closure to year...

ENJOY ALL THE SEASONS OF YOUR LIFE.

In conclusion...

No matter how favorable the land... no matter how capable the winemaker, attempting to grow a varietal in an area incompatible with the nature of the grape will produce less than perfect results.

When we find ourselves in life situations demanding we work out of realms contrary to our nature, our results will be the same.

We may even actually be very adept at something we don't particularly enjoy doing, but the energy it requires to produce these results can prove exhausting.

When we find our 'niche' - that place where things flow - the whole world can seem a lot friendlier. This, of course, is not a new concept. "Follow your bliss", "Do What You Love and the Money Will Follow"... And then you ALSO have " I Could Do Anything If Only I Knew What It Was". *

So knowing more about your "Inner Grape" can lead you to a path where the energy will flow more naturally. Then you will hopefully either discover, uncover or resuscitate activities, lifestyles and career moves that will be a natural part of who you are meant to be.

Cheers and keep on sipping!
Maureen

> *"Twenty years from now you will be more disappointed by the things you didn't do than by the ones you did do. So throw off the bowlines. Sail away from the safe harbor. Catch the trade winds in your sails.*
> *Explore. Dream. Discover."*
> – Mark Twain

Enjoy the journey.

* "Follow Your Bliss": General Formula for students of Joseph Campbell - The Power of Myth

Do What You Love And The Money Will Follow: Marsha Sinetar

I Could Do Anything If Only I Knew What It Was: Barbara Sher

Tread lightly upon this earth.
The impressions made with our heart
will be those
not washed away
by the sands of time...
Tread lightly.
Love deeply.

- *Maureen*

WINE TYPES: The Seminar.

Looking for a non-traditional Wine Tasting event? "Wine Types: Discover Your Inner Grape" may be just what you are looking for. Whether you need a fun, educational ice-breaker to kick off a longer convention or just a "different" way to celebrate the social aspect of wine tasting, this could be just the seminar for you!

So... are you
A Pinot Noir?
A Cabernet?
A Champagne?
A Merlot?

Nature vs. Nurture...
"Terroir" vs. winemaker influence...

Just as we are born with certain personality characteristics, we are then influenced by our environment. "WINE TYPES" is a way of looking at who we are - and which wine varietal we most resemble.

DISCOVER YOUR INNER GRAPE.

WINE TYPES: The Seminar
Fun, Educational, Vintage.

For more info, contact Maureen:
sage workshops
(360) 371-7466
sagebutterfly2@comcast.net

Be sure to visit **www.vintagesentiments.com** to view a wide variety of wine greeting cards, Wine Types merchandise, to order additional copies of Wine Types or to find out more about "Wine Types - The Seminar."

About the author....

Maureen Kelly has been involved in teaching interpersonal communication concepts for over 18 years. As a seminar leader, Yoga teacher and Heart Rhythm Meditation instructor, her goal is to offer workshops that "move your body, move your mind and move your spirit."

Animals are also a huge part of her life and she loves and respects them for what they teach us.

She currently sips her wine in beautiful Birch Bay, Washington, where she shares her abode with numerous 4-leggeds.

If you have any questions or comments you would like to share, you can email her at: sagebutterfly2@comcast.net.

Recommended Reading

Personality / Communication
Gifts Differing - Isabel Briggs Myers
Type Talk - Otto Kroeger & Janet Thuesen
Still True to Type - William C Jeffries
Please Understand Me - David Keirsey & Marilyn Bates

Enlightenment
Inspiration: Your Ultimate Calling - Dr. Wayne Dyer
Unconditional Life - Deepak Chopra
The Four Agreements - Don Miguel Ruiz
Tuesdays With Morrie - Mitch Albom
The Untethered Soul - Michael A. Singer
Energize Your Heart - Puran & Susanna Bair

Animal Behavior & Communication
Kinship with All Life - J. Allen Boone
The Language of Miracles - Amelia Kinkade

Fun & Wonderful
Marley & Me - John Grogan
Can't Wait To Get To Heaven - Fannie Flagg
Eat, Pray, Love - Elizabeth Gilbert

... and oh so many more...

Extra Wine Types Assessments

Check the boxes on the following pages that most closely describe you.

CATEGORY 1 - ORDER

☐ Punctuality is very important to me.

☐ I tend to be very orderly.

☐ My friends know they can depend on me.

☐ I study the pros and cons before decision-making.

☐ I love to make lists and cross things off.

☐ I take commitments seriously.

☐ I enjoy detail work.

☐ I like to belong to clubs & organizations.

☐ I appreciate a structured environment.

☐ My motto could be "If it ain't broke, don't fix it."

☐ I follow Murphy's Law... if it can go wrong, it probably will.

☐ I am not crazy about change.

Total boxes checked: _____

CATEGORY 2 - RISK

- [ ] I adapt easily to new situations.
- [ ] I tend to live in the "now" and don't much like plans.
- [ ] I am a negotiator by nature.
- [ ] I get bored easily.
- [ ] I enjoy a fast pace.
- [ ] I'm not crazy about commitment.
- [ ] I like to take risks.
- [ ] I am good at putting out fires and enjoy the challenge.
- [ ] I sometimes appear unpredictable.
- [ ] I handle emergency situations well.
- [ ] I tend to be impulsive.
- [ ] I may have 10 things going at once, but am not always great with completion of task.
- [ ] I am a "free spirit".

Total boxes checked: _____

CATEGORY 3 - INDEPENDENCE

- ☐ I value independence.
- ☐ I am a skeptic by nature.
- ☐ I can appear cool or arrogant.
- ☐ No matter how good something is, I can improve on it.
- ☐ The conception of an idea is more fun than the follow through.
- ☐ I seek competence in myself and others.
- ☐ I have an unquenchable thirst for knowledge.
- ☐ I say "change for the sake of change!"
- ☐ If I see a button, I'll probably push it. ("Wonder what THIS does?")
- ☐ I'm always asking why...
- ☐ I enjoy playing devil's advocate.
- ☐ I am intrigued by a good riddle.
- ☐ I work well with ideas and concepts.

Total boxes checked: _____

CATEGORY 4 - ALTRUISM

- [ ] I am normally a good listener.
- [ ] I am an idealist by nature.
- [ ] I would like to make a difference in the world.
- [ ] I am drawn to careers that help people.
- [ ] Conflict makes me very uneasy.
- [ ] I am sensitive to criticism.
- [ ] I want to please "all the people all the time."
- [ ] I say "yes" sometimes when I really feel like saying "no".
- [ ] I search for the meaning of life.
- [ ] I am good at generating alternatives.
- [ ] I enjoy artistic endeavors: acting, writing, etc.
- [ ] I am prone to daydreaming.
- [ ] I don't like dealing with detail.

Total boxes checked: _____

Check the boxes on the following pages that most closely describe you.

CATEGORY 1 - ORDER

☐ Punctuality is very important to me.

☐ I tend to be very orderly.

☐ My friends know they can depend on me.

☐ I study the pros and cons before decision-making.

☐ I love to make lists and cross things off.

☐ I take commitments seriously.

☐ I enjoy detail work.

☐ I like to belong to clubs & organizations.

☐ I appreciate a structured environment.

☐ My motto could be "If it ain't broke, don't fix it."

☐ I follow Murphy's Law... if it can go wrong, it probably will.

☐ I am not crazy about change.

Total boxes checked: _____

CATEGORY 2 - RISK

- [ ] I adapt easily to new situations.
- [ ] I tend to live in the "now" and don't much like plans.
- [ ] I am a negotiator by nature.
- [ ] I get bored easily.
- [ ] I enjoy a fast pace.
- [ ] I'm not crazy about commitment.
- [ ] I like to take risks.
- [ ] I am good at putting out fires and enjoy the challenge.
- [ ] I sometimes appear unpredictable.
- [ ] I handle emergency situations well.
- [ ] I tend to be impulsive.
- [ ] I may have 10 things going at once, but am not always great with completion of task.
- [ ] I am a "free spirit".

Total boxes checked: _____

CATEGORY 3 - INDEPENDENCE

- [ ] I value independence.
- [ ] I am a skeptic by nature.
- [ ] I can appear cool or arrogant.
- [ ] No matter how good something is, I can improve on it.
- [ ] The conception of an idea is more fun than the follow through.
- [ ] I seek competence in myself and others.
- [ ] I have an unquenchable thirst for knowledge.
- [ ] I say "change for the sake of change!"
- [ ] If I see a button, I'll probably push it. ("Wonder what THIS does?")
- [ ] I'm always asking why...
- [ ] I enjoy playing devil's advocate.
- [ ] I am intrigued by a good riddle.
- [ ] I work well with ideas and concepts.

Total boxes checked: _____

CATEGORY 4 - ALTRUISM

▪ I am normally a good listener.

▪ I am an idealist by nature.

▪ I would like to make a difference in the world.

▪ I am drawn to careers that help people.

▪ Conflict makes me very uneasy.

▪ I am sensitive to criticism.

▪ I want to please "all the people all the time."

▪ I say "yes" sometimes when I really feel like saying "no".

▪ I search for the meaning of life.

▪ I am good at generating alternatives.

▪ I enjoy artistic endeavors: acting, writing, etc.

▪ I am prone to daydreaming.

▪ I don't like dealing with detail.

Total boxes checked: _____

In Vino, Veritas.

ROOM FOR YOUR OWN NOTES...

www.ingramcontent.com/pod-product-compliance
Lightning Source LLC
LaVergne TN
LVHW011735060526
838200LV00051B/3174